MINDSET MATTERS MOST

**How to Create Success &
Happiness by Releasing from the**

FEAR, LIMITATIONS & SELF-DOUBT

That Hold You Back...

Brian J. Grasso

Carrie, Chase & Miyah

Be you. Happy comes first. Serve others.

That is all.

CONTENTS

FOREWORD

The founder of the Mindset Performance Institute and creator of the "Awaken Your Freedom" movement, Brian Grasso has established himself as the epitome of mindset. Now he returns with the magnum opus of his life's work, *Mindset Matters Most*. This masterpiece will set you free as he teaches you how to release your fears, limitations, and self-doubt in a practical way.

When I was approached by Brian and asked to write the foreword of his new book, I was speechless. I was seriously honored to take part in such a profound piece of literature.

I've read *Mindset Matters Most* and I can firmly say that it is a true masterpiece. This book just flows from start to finish.

I have been involved in mindset my entire life. In addition to having a master's degree in psychology, I have written a bestseller entitled *The Mind Body Solution*. It's safe to say that I've read countless books on mindset, psychology, and human behavior.

I must note that, out of all of the books I've read, *Mindset Matters Most* is the pinnacle of this beautiful area of study.

I've known Brian for many years, and I have seen firsthand the power of practicing his own mindset strategies. Brian and I became very close over the past few months; I have had the honor of becoming his business coach and helping him grow his brand on a global level.

In working with Brian personally, I was able to witness the massive growth of his #MindsetMattersMost movement, which is taking the world by storm.

Now more than ever, his message is needed. I am beyond grateful to coach Brian and share his incredible talents and impact more lives around the world.

Working in close proximity to Brian, I have witnessed firsthand how aligned he is with his philosophy. Brian most definitely talks the talk and walks the walk. He is truly an enigma; he has changed many lives and no doubt will transform many more.

This book will shift your life in a profound way and I highly suggest you read it many times. It is the kind of book that keeps on giving; you will gain new insights each time you re-read the wisdom contained in these pages.

Share this book with as many friends and family members as possible. You will be giving them the gift of total transformation.

I myself am taken aback by the exceptional writing in this book and the powerful message that will live on for centuries to come.

Mindset Matters Most is timeless, as are all of the concepts that Brian shares.

I'm certain that you will get as much value from it as I did.

All I ask of you is to read this book with an open mind and allow yourself to be guided by the reins of your heart.

With Love,

AJ Mihrzad

Author, *The Mind Body Solution: Train Your Brain for Permanent Weight Loss*

Founder, OnlineSupercoach.com

INTRODUCTION

The mind is everything.

What you think, you become.

—Buddha

You currently live within the defined boundaries of two separate boxes.

The large, outermost box is solid-lined and represents the factors in your world that are immoveable. You had no role in creating the box, have no immediate cause-and-effect ability to challenge its borders, and remain bound by its authority over you.

The much smaller, inner box has perforated lines and involves elements that are completely in your control to change. You built the box of your own accord, can alter its dimensions at your whim, and completely own the space both within and around it.

No, you can't overcome depression tomorrow.

No, you can't lose twenty pounds in seven days healthfully.

No, you can't go from bankruptcy to millionaire overnight.

No, you can't summon what you want by merely thinking about it flowing to you.

And shame on the people in this world who use the truly magical realities of manifestation, attraction, or divine inspiration to claim that you can.

But yes, you can become happier today.

Yes, you can begin the process of establishing a healthy lifestyle immediately.

Yes, you can create a more sustainable cash flow quickly.

Yes, you can simplify your work and enjoy the journey of achieving your goals.

And shame on the people in this world who teach a cynical brand of reality to claim that you can't.

Your thoughts have created the self-imposed limitations of that perforated box.

This book will give you the tools to push the confines of that box permanently.

It doesn't matter if your goal is related to health, fitness, love, relationships, money, happiness, or career endeavors.

The undeniable first step to success in anything is mindset.

As your mindset goes, so goes your life.

Simply "ACCEPT" that a different reality
is possible...

SECTION 1: ACCEPTANCE

*The acts of a man spring from the hidden
seeds of his thoughts...*

—Earl Nightingale

Part 1

It seems odd for a health, fitness, and wellness professional to say they're depressed.

Almost counterintuitive.

After all, these are the energetic, happy-go-lucky, motivational, and high-on-life sorts who present a vibrant face to the world while advocating the mental and emotional benefits of a lifestyle rich in quality food and consistent exercise.

But you may be surprised to learn that most health, fitness, and wellness professionals I know have experienced deep sadness at one point of their lives or another.

No matter how spirited they showcase themselves as on social media.

And in case you were curious...

I was one of them.

For nearly twenty years, I was known as one of the most successful and acclaimed health, fitness, and wellness professionals on the planet.

I had been a performance coach for collegiate, national team, professional, and Olympic athletes throughout North America.

I traveled the world as a guest lecturer and consultant, wrote for well-known industry magazines such as *Men's Fitness*, was profiled for my work in major media outlets, and even served as an advisor for Nike.

And yet, for the first decade of that twenty-year stint, I was gripped by the cold hands and encircling darkness of a depression that nearly took my life.

My diagnoses ranged from clinical depression and bipolar to PTSD and seasonal affective disorder, depending on which specialist I saw.

The prescribed solution was always a combination of psychotherapy and medication.

Neither of which I ever partook in.

The thing is, there was no specific cause or traumatic event that I could remember, necessarily.

I was just sad.

Some days mildly.

Other days, so completely that it consumed every single breath I took and made the very action of getting out of bed feel insurmountable.

Can you relate?

According to the most recent Harris Poll, only one in three Americans defined themselves as happy. That means that more than 200 million people would not.

This statistical reality extends worldwide and most certainly is not contained to this continent.

The subjective nature of measuring happiness remains complex, but the underscored simplicity is something we have become numb to. If the true object of happiness is to be happy for no reason, then how often do we mistakenly associate a "good" occurrence with the justification to be happy?

And, most certainly, vice versa.

In our commonality as human beings, my "health, fitness, and wellness professional" classification is irrelevant.

The central point is an unmistakable experience we all share: knowing exactly what it feels like to smile while suppressing the sadness.

No matter how mild or all-consuming it may be.

Part 2

For me, the slide into a dark hole started around the age of seventeen.

Unexpectedly.

I remember that it began with what could best be described as a general malaise.

Pockets of time where 'sadness' just seemed to kick in out of nowhere and ranged on the spectrum from slightly numbing to complete envelopment.

And if I were forced to give a description to "complete envelopment," I would simply say this:

I was in a very deep, dark hole that seemed impossible to climb out of.

A void so profound, it often felt like it was going to swallow me from the inside.

I trudged through my senior year of high school and every day of college in this perennial, albeit unpredictable, state.

Some days, I managed to smile because the overwhelming gloom was reasonable.

Other days, the suffocation was so intense and so purely impossible, I'm not unconvinced that perfect strangers on public transit could see through and actually sense my despair.

During it all, the overriding emotion was loneliness.

It remains, to this day, the single emotion that haunts me.

Living in a city of four million and constantly surrounded by friends, colleagues, and family seems an unimaginable place to experience solitude.

But if you've walked in my shoes—which I'm convinced most have, even for a short period of time—you know just how much that improbability is true.

For nearly a decade, I didn't live.

I existed.

Survived.

And I suppose that's where the irony sets in full force.

Part 3

Because in this hollow, barren place where breathing on some days felt laborious, my "job" was to be the air of inspiration for my clients.

Their beacon of light.

The very reason they themselves would begrudgingly get out of bed at five a.m. after heeding my call that the mental and emotional benefits of regular exercise were even more profoundly important than the physical enhancements they'd see.

"Putting on" became my life.

At many points in my early career, I often felt as though an Academy Award should have been offered for the way I finessed my outer facade against the backdrop of my internal struggle.

And that's where I think most everyone— including you—can relate heavily.

Everyone's walk through depression or sadness is different.

I don't know if there is a uniform way in which we experience that world.

But I do know that, for most of the people I've ever spoken with candidly about this topic, the duality of the brave face and manufactured enthusiasm is where there is the most common ground amongst us.

We feel like frauds.

Living two lives.

Not always certain what's wrong.

But always uncertain of how to fix it.

Perhaps the most tragic, lonely, isolating, suffocating, and crushing experience any one of us could possibly imagine.

And I don't believe there is "an answer," a system, intervention, or blueprint for how to "solve," "cure," or "fix" it. I believe that varying things work for varying people.

But I can tell you what worked for me and, inevitably, what became the staging point for developing a success-driven, inspired, and happy mindset that now has me seeing the world through the innocent eyes of a child intent on believing that anything is possible.

I forced myself to learn about the nature of reality.

And for a long while, it was very much a forced effort.

Because there were days that getting out of bed to brush my teeth felt more overwhelming than may seem reasonable to you.

I read one page of a book.

Then three.

A chapter.

Then five.

Over time—and it certainly took time—I began to reshape my understanding of the world.

Of myself.

Of reality.

Removing esoteric, metaphysical, or confusing rhetoric, what I came to understand is that the reality I was experiencing wasn't reality.

It was "a" reality. The chosen reality I saw, felt, and lived.

And that one spark of comprehension was all it took.

I did not "fight," "warrior-up," or "combat" anything. Through the years, I learned that when I did that—when "fight" became my story—it only served to intensify the dark clouds around me by perpetuating a struggle.

Instead, I allowed.

Calmly.

I allowed myself, my brain, to start accepting the possibility that there were other "realities" in life.

That perhaps I wasn't suffering as the victim of my thoughts and emotions, as much as I was simply not yet engineering them in the direction I could.

Yes, all is blissful now. But not because my circumstances changed. Because my thoughts and emotions did.

And not by chance.

But because I summoned them to.

That's the journey it took for me to deeply understand just how much "Mindset Matters Most."

For everything:

Your happiness.

Relationships.

Fitness and health.

Business success.

Financial success.

Beyond and then some.

Part 4

Maybe you connect deeply to my own experiences of walking through sadness.

Maybe not.

But Section 2 of this book will help you understand that the reason we often plod through life without truly chasing our dreams, being happy for no reason and living to our highest potential, is based simply on how little we know ourselves.

Intimately.

We often seek external motivation to fire us up, perform acts of kindness to fill us up, and attend personal or professional development seminars to raise us up, but we rarely seem to be able to make any of that sustainable.

The motivational fires extinguish no sooner than they spark.

The sense of gratification for doing good often fades quickly.

The ascension leads to an abrupt, sometimes painful fall.

It's as if an unknown, unseen force is keeping us stuck, intent on preventing, if not defeating, our desires or attempts to achieve more, do more, and become more. A vicious cycle that feels like the terrifying paralysis of drowning slowly in shallow waters.

Which brings me to a metaphor that truly helped open my eyes along the journey.

It opened my eyes because of how clearly it shows just how much we look in the wrong direction for the answers.

The wrong direction and entirely incorrect channels.

It's been written and said by countless people in countless ways that in order to create real, lasting change, we need to look no further than ourselves.

That all the strength we'd ever need, inspiration we'd ever want, or bliss we'd ever feel is contained neatly within us. A literal volcano of potential that requires a simple spark to unleash.

But to those who, like me, have spent more than one night of their lives curled up in a ball of sorrow, skin raw and dry from the endless tears that had been shed and wondering if their loved ones would be far better off without them, that kind of motivational rhetoric doesn't penetrate as factual.

In truth, it makes us feel more broken.

As if there is a great secret of inspired living that the rest of the world seems to understand and apply with ease, but we can't crack the code.

Part 5

This simple analogy helped me begin the process of unraveling it all:

You're standing in a rowboat, admiring the sublime view on the horizon. The calm sea, warm breeze, and dipping sunset call to you daily. That's your dream: To stop looking at the oasis and start living within its embrace.

You pick up the oar with great excitement, set a goal to be living on those open waters by a certain date, and begin to row.

At first, you row with enthusiasm and optimism. Surely this time your technique will cause the oar to hit the water in just the right way and at just the right cadence to propel you into that dream life.

But it takes no time for the optimism to vanish because, yet again, you find yourself going nowhere. Memories of past failure begin building in your gut and bring with them a welling of emotion that carries the label "not me."

The haunting pit of a feeling that you've experienced before—no matter how many times you've desperately tried to ignore it—that surrounds you and makes you believe success and happiness don't comprise your destiny.

That you aren't worthy.

So you do what the standard societal idioms of our time convince you to do.

You search for the will and determination to row harder.

You read the motivational slogans, consult the motivational videos, and even hire your very own motivational coach. The one who tells you that if you REALLY want it and you REALLY want to live in the majesty of those open waters, than you REALLY have to put your nose to the grindstone and hustle.

But the increased motivation provides no traction. In fact, the harder you row, the more tired you get and the less you move from the spot you're in.

Defeated, you turn your attention towards other people who you see trying to row.

Perhaps a more charitable, less self-centered approach is what's needed to get your boat on its path. After all, from the school system to religion and politics, we're conditioned to both believe and accept that helping and guiding others should be our primary objective in life and that, in doing so, the action of aiding others will be of benefit to our own goals.

Full of altruism, you begin offering advice.

Motivation.

And key insights that will help others get their boats in gear.

It feels good at first, but then you come to realize something profound.

Well-intentioned or not, your advice is of little use. Your motivation, completely artificial. Your insights, entirely cosmetic.

If you knew how to get a boat into those wondrous open waters, then you wouldn't be stuck at the shore yourself. Moreover, the more you try to help, the less focus you place on your own journey.

Dejected, you decide to investigate different methods of rowing.

Perhaps you simply lack the knowledge of how to get your oar angled properly. It's not so much that you don't have the dream life squarely in sight or that you don't have the motivation to truly do the work to make it happen; you just aren't sure the exact cause-and-effect relationship of how to get the oar and the water to work in unison.

Feeling roused by your epiphany, you begin looking into the "how to" books, purchase the "how to" programs, and even hire your very own "how to" coach. The one who helps you understand the finer points of rowing and simplifies the process for you.

But the improved knowledge you've gained offers no success. In fact, the more you learn about how to row, the more confused you become and the less you move from the spot you're in.

Broken, you opt to start the process of creating better self-talk.

Maybe by stating positive affirmations, you can spiritually seduce your boat to move. The vision of the dream life isn't the problem. Nor is the motivation, or the desire you have to help others, culpable for why you only ever managed to fight a current that seems determined to keep you at shore.

You simply need to call upon the mystical, supernatural forces of our universe. To align with them and allow them to part the waters on your behalf.

With renewed faith, you begin telling yourself that you can. You recite "you can" mantras, chant "you can" prayers, and even hire your very own "you can" coach. The one who tells you that "you can," even when you lose belief in yourself.

But all the "you can" talk doesn't prove worthy. In fact, the more you say "you can" in the absence of your boat actually cruising, the more you reinforce "you can't" and the less you move from the spot you're in.

The cycle complete, you now feel hopeless.

Goal setting had little effect.

Searching for external motivation had little impact.

Helping others while you can barely stay afloat had little value.

Altering your self-talk had little outcome.

Part 6

"Linchpin" is one of my favorite words of all time.

Every time I see the word or think of it, I conjure the same mental image.

The linchpin is the thing we can't always see.

Most of the time because we're simply facing the wrong direction.

It's not so much that it isn't in plain sight; we just get caught up in the other, more visible factors of the panorama, so seldom notice it.

But the linchpin is the thing that makes everything else work.

It doesn't typically have the sex appeal or visual allure of all the other parts of a given equation—which is why we overlook it so profoundly—but when we do draw our eyes in its direction, we uncover a limitless ocean of power.

Fine-tune the linchpin, the entire instrument plays at perfect pitch.

Ignore the linchpin, the cacophony of noise pierces us at the core in the most harsh and cutting ways imaginable.

For the purpose of the rowboat metaphor, the linchpin is a small thread of rope.

The rope that keeps your boat tied to the dock.

Your desire to be in the breathtaking waters, effort to create goals that take you there, hunting of external motivation to fire you up, desire to place others' journey ahead of your own, and attempts to affirm your worthiness to make it all happen combine to create the illusion of success.

But, in truth, you go nowhere unless that rope is untied.

In life, that rope is your mindset.

Leave it tied in knots, your desires toward love, happiness, career, money, and fitness will forever elude you.

Learn to untangle its bond, your boat will simply be picked up by a current that already knows the way and will most certainly take you to that vista of your dreams.

Success and happiness are not about learning how to become successful and happy.

They're about releasing from the reasons you're not.

Which is why I'll say again:

There is an unknown, unseen force keeping you stuck. Intent on preventing, if not defeating, your desires or attempts to achieve more, do more, and become more.

That's the linchpin.

Change your mindset, everything changes with it.

Part 7

At the apex of the depression, my very best friend was an oak tree.

A large, looming piece of timber that stood in our neighbor's yard and directly in front of the second-story bedroom window of my parents' home that was my cocoon.

I suppose, in retrospect, that "cocoon" is a fitting word, given that it was this rather small and intimate twelve-by-twelve place in which my ascension from anguished spirit to inspired soul began. But in truth, it better represents the state of my outlook at the time.

From my bedroom I was insulated from the paralyzing fears that sat in threatening wait just outside the door.

Those fears were not real in substance, necessarily, but very much so in clout.

I would sit for hours in front of that window watching young children breeze by on their bikes with smiles infused with glee and unintentionally mocking my sorrow. I could never understand why they were so happy and I wasn't.

Urban professionals walked at a determined, enthusiastic pace to their purposeful jobs with a sense of excitement that caused envy and spite to well up inside me. I could never understand why they lived with such passion and I didn't.

But mostly, I looked at that massive oak tree.

At least a century old, it served as the constant in my agony-filled world.

It saw me wipe away the single tears.

It watched me weep uncontrollably.

It was there when the cold hollowness penetrated so deeply, crying wasn't an option.

As far as I could tell, the window, my torment, and that oak tree were to be my reality forever.

Not long ago, I visited my parents.

They still live in the same house where I grew up.

My old room looked surprisingly the same, but the view from that window, completely different.

Young children were breezing by on their bikes and I smiled with them.

Urban professionals walked enthusiastically and I shared their sense of passion.

The oak tree is gone.

Cut down, according to my dad, years ago.

And as I stared through my window, I couldn't help but notice how different the view looked.

Without the mighty presence of that oak tree, the panorama seemed limitless.

Blue skies.

Endless horizon.

A whole new perspective on the world.

There is seldom an easy answer when it comes to changing the view of your life.

But the hope I can offer is that it is possible.

I wasn't broken, defective, beyond repair, or damaged goods. And neither are you.

All I needed was a different perspective. And so do you.

Suffering and that oak tree was my reality.

Reality can change.

And once you accept that, the remaining portions of this book will provide you the solution.

Part 8

I've spent a great deal of time writing about my years of depression.

But the very same perspective shift that allowed me to shed that burden also speaks to how I transitioned so many other areas of my life, as well.

In 2001, I came within inches of having to declare bankruptcy.

This happened shortly after finalizing a bitter divorce that left me temporarily homeless and emotionally gutted.

It was right around the same time that my weight soared to an unhealthy lifetime high of 280 pounds.

I know the bottom of the barrel very well and on many levels.

And I'm more than familiar with that innate frustration of knowing you're worth more than this, but just can't seem to make any of it work. You know what to do, but just can't assemble the energy or will to do it with conviction.

At least not sustainably. Like a kite in a windstorm, you may be at the mercy of circumstances that seem outside your control without knowing from day to day if your mood, belief, or self-worth is going to be calm and true or harsh and unsteady.

Yes, I used proper measures of training and nutrition to lose some weight.

I had a few short-lived, empty relationships.

I made some money through a hustle and grind mentality.

But none of it lasted.

My weight rebounded.

My emotional walls were too high for meaningful connections.

My self-worth was too low for viable businesses to profit.

What made everything change—permanently—was when I stopped trying to fix each individual issue with a Band-Aid or look at them as isolated, separate situations.

The single thread that connected these seemingly unconnected adversities was my perspective.

My mindset.

Life is a walking representation of the perspective we carry. Perspective we carry of ourselves, our potential, our worth, our ability, and our circumstances.

Perspectives, by definition, are not true in the material sense. They are merely opinions. Current opinions, which can be swayed and changed in time.

Nothing of me today resembles me of my past.

Not in health, fitness, relationships, money, happiness, spiritual connectedness, or any other quantifier of success you could think of.

Perspective is that powerful. In both the positive and negative sense. It can allow you to see a vast ocean of possibility or a myopic viewpoint the size of a pea. The only determinant?

What you choose to see.

Part 9

I never used to believe I had a choice.

And I'm fairly certain that you don't believe it, either.

Whether entombed by a dark sadness, desperate to find the love of your life, wanting to finally see your business idea deliver you into financial freedom, step into the brilliance of a peaceful, happy existence, lose weight, or locate the resolve to chase down that dream job, I know that having someone tell you it's all just a matter of choice can be infuriating.

But the truth is, not only do you have the power to choose, you *are* choosing.

Success in any avenue has nothing to do with luck, serendipity, chance, or situational fortune. It's simply the outcome of choices you make every day. The perceptions you carry become the belief systems you hold, which in turn create the expectations you have.

Those expectations drive your actions, habits, and behaviors at all times.

When I was overweight, finding diet, exercise, and even motivational solutions to the problem was very easy.

But I did not perceive myself as a fit, lean man. Which meant that I did not believe I had the ability to follow a guided fitness regimen. Which meant that I did not expect to succeed.

So no matter how quality the instruction I was receiving, how rich the motivation, how much willpower, grit, or self-discipline I tried to incorporate, the inevitable would always happen.

I would self-sabotage.

And I would do so without really knowing why I was. I ate foods that I knew I shouldn't and grew increasingly annoyed at myself. I skipped workouts I knew I couldn't and created excuses for why I wasn't able to get them in.

The more I sabotaged my own efforts and claims of desire, the more I ended up proving to myself that I was not worthy of achieving them. That no matter what, I simply wouldn't succeed. Which made my perspective even more negatively unwavering and staunch.

I *was* choosing my destiny.

I just didn't realize I was. Much the same as you don't realize you are.

That's because the true mechanism of choice doesn't reside in our conscious brain. That unknown, unseen force keeping you stuck, intent on preventing, if not defeating, your desires or attempts to achieve more, do more, and become more is your unconscious mind.

The silent powerhouse that dictates your life.

The literal engine of your mindset.

As it goes, so go your actions, habits, and behaviors every day.

Either aligned and bringing you closer to what you want for your life, or disjointed and taking you farther away.

Part 10

In many ways, your mindset is given to you.

Through the years, your accumulated influences and experiences converge to build the metaphysical eyes from which you see. Those influences range from cultural and societal ones that you may not even realize exist to social and environmental ones that begin in early childhood and perpetually act upon you for life.

With every influence, experience, and subsequent reaction or outcome, a snapshot is taken by the unconscious and used as a blueprint going forward. Labels such as people-pleaser, failure, overcomer, winner, over-thinker, and victim are identities that many people worldwide can relate to as the core of "who" they are.

When the compass of your unconscious is set to any identity, the nature of your experiences and outcomes of your adventures in life always seem to follow the basic overtone of that identity.

You're the girl who has it all and everything seems to work for you with ease.

You're the guy who has nothing and everything seems to become a disaster.

Or, perhaps, life is a combination of those two extremes.

However closely you choose to connect to your identity, your daily actions, habits, and behaviors will be driven by that story; associated results will follow.

But "who" you are is not nearly an absolute.

It's merely the identity you're choosing to carry at the moment, which has been afforded you through influence, reinforced by perception, adopted as a belief system, and held as an expectation.

The first order of business, then, in untying your rope, loosening the knot, and releasing yourself from that dock keeping you stuck in life is simply to accept that it's all just a story.

That who you are, what you're capable of, and where your potential lives are not remotely absolute truths. They are constructs of your perspective and, no matter how reinforced they may appear due to the social proof of your life, they do not represent the only vision of reality.

Just the one you're currently choosing to see and experience.

Part 11

Simply "ACCEPT" that a different reality is possible.

With your love-life, finances, fitness, health, career, or entrepreneurial efforts.

You don't even have to have faith or belief (yet) that your new reality is just around the corner. In fact, I'd advise that you don't (more on that in Section 4).

You merely need to create a platform of acceptance.

Consider yourself a camera sitting atop a tripod in the middle of a massive room. Your perspective is contained to a very limited viewpoint. The room itself is full of wonder, awe-inspiring potential, and unlimited possibility, but you have become fixed to a stationary position. Through that small window of the camera lens, you have created a story and conviction that this angle of the room is the only angle that exists.

Unless someone were to move the tripod.

Then the story would change.

A brand new vantage point would become accessible.

Illumination would grow where only darkness and ignorance lived before.

And that's the beginning of how it all changes.

My sincerest hope is that with Section 1, I moved your tripod...

"I see you," he repeated...

SECTION 2: AWARENESS

What is necessary to create change is to change one's awareness of self.

—Abraham Maslow

Part 12

Spinach.

That's what I remember most about the night that changed my life.

I understand that stories like this usually start off with some kind of compelling saga that reads like a Hollywood script.

A situation, circumstance, or event that involves a near-death experience or awe-inspiring feat that explains why the storyteller's entire life course changed in a single instant.

But I've always believed that there is more beauty and power in the small, everyday occurrences we all share than most seem to give credit to.

And the very reason that re-directing your life path into the oasis that you so desperately want it to be really doesn't require anything outside of a small spark.

A simple flash of clarity or blink of hope that helps you realize the life you've had doesn't have to be the life you have.

Which is why I was quietly grateful that I had declined the chef's suggestion of adding olive oil to the fresh spinach underneath my perfectly cooked piece of Atlantic salmon.

The natural, earthy taste of the greens combined flawlessly with the buttery texture of the fish.

It remains but one of the many senses I have remembered with clear fascination from my dinner on the outdoor terrace of a restaurant in Melbourne, Australia, not so many years ago.

Life-changing moments have a way of staying entrenched in your brain.

Even the smallest detail.

I found the chill in the night air particularly annoying — likely the result of a North American raised man unprepared for the sting of winter in August.

The gas-powered lamp to my left cast a peculiar, flickering shadow over our table of six and was forcing one side of my body to drip with an aggravating perspiration while the other side sat frozen in the oddity of a mid-summer frost.

And of course, there was Douglas.

A positively jovial character with twinkling eyes, rosy cheeks, and the type of devilish, wily grin that revealed a certain playful, if not mischievous, nature.

Picture Santa but 150 pounds lighter, with short brown hair and without the red suit.

As he spoke, it became clear that the scamp-like image I had crafted was terribly mistaken.

Here sat the most intensely awakened man I had ever come across.

Wildly soulful, with a depth that was both unmistakable and stunning.

So madly alive.

Douglas understood people.

The human experience.

Our collective journey through life.

A planet of nearly seven billion souls, all of whom live with the extreme terror of isolation and sadness from time to time, however contradictory that may seem.

His insight and piercing gaze left me naked and realizing that I had been skimming the surface my entire existence.

The great secret to life was a simple relic of ancient wisdom.

Something that our fast-paced, numbers-oriented, material-centric world absolutely could embrace, if we were to be so inclined.

The woody taste of the spinach lingered lightly on my tongue.

The icy air calmed.

The heat lamp became soothing.

"Sawubona," he said.

I felt alive.

For the first time in my life.

Part 13

The roar of the engine just outside my window combined in unforgiving disharmony with the all-too-common loud talker stationed two rows up and one row diagonal from where I sat.

I leaned my head against the window in a veiled attempt to stuff my six-foot-two frame comfortably into the plane seat that would carry me for the next thirteen hours.

Melbourne to Chicago was no easy trek for one riddled with this much soulful discomfort.

It had been two days since my incredible encounter with Douglas.

Two very sleepless and impossibly irritating nights.

But my anxiety was not the sort that resulted from usual societal patterns of stress.

The typical daily worries and dread that seem to plague us all—money, health, love, or the busyness of mundane task management.

This was much deeper and made me realize how incredibly superficial and artificial our everyday battles truly are.

Almost as if we create drama and strain out of necessity to help us avoid the most pressing and authentic question of all:

"Who am I, really?"

Outside the label that explains what you "do" for a living.

The box that seems to define what you can or cannot become.

The self-limiting definitions that contain you—even condemn you—to merely going from one day to the next, existing on auto-pilot.

Partially happy.

Occasionally fulfilled.

Somewhat content.

But only when you don't think about it.

Because when you do, the emptiness and grief can become too overwhelming.

"Language has become such an informality in our society," he said with deep conviction.

I was recalling Douglas's wisdom and the conversation I had been blessed to be part of two nights previous.

"We walk through life with our heads down, as if afraid to make eye contact or acknowledge each other, even non-verbally," he continued.

I silently agreed.

Many times in my life, I had noticed the minute details on the faces and in the energy of the people I was passing on crowded streets while navigating a humdrum, barren world of my own.

People engrossed in their private stresses. Expressions either fixed in scowl-like grief, entirely devoid of emotion, or putting on a brave front to mask the internal struggle they have as a constant companion.

"Much worse," Douglas's spirited voice and vivacious presence brought me back to the moment.

"When we do actually converse, it's trivial. Friendly, but abrupt and empty."

I silently objected.

Long considered a "tree-hugging hippie" by those who knew me best, I have always had faith in humankind.

Always believing, however naïvely, that the world is comprised of people who care more than they may show.

Douglas turned his charming gaze in my direction and met my eyes with a fierce yet effervescent expression.

Had he somehow cosmically heard my dissenting thoughts?

"You disagree?" he asked with an alluring kindness.

"Not in principle, but in practice," I offered back through a relaxed smile.

"Explain," he countered calmly.

"Well, people are most certainly busy. Between career, family, and the everyday stress of deadlines, traffic, and bills, we are all very pressed for time and tend to have a restricted mental economy — that is, our interactions, by necessity, must be kept rather short. I think perhaps you are confusing indifference with the need for brevity."

I immediately began wondering if my defensiveness for humanity at large was much more about shielding myself from the truth I had been living.

A cloak of mediocrity that I had willing slung around my own shoulders.

Playing the victim, using my daily burdens as fair reasoning for why I didn't reach out more often, love freely, or put the service of others at least equal in status with my own needs.

Part 14

"Let me ask you this, Brian," Douglas said with the rousing excitement of a man set to declare checkmate.

"If you were walking down the street and passed someone you know—let's say this person is a casual friend—and you could clearly see that they were visibly distraught or emotionally shaken in some way, what would you do?"

I was beginning to feel like a loveless villain.

"I would ask them how they are," I said meekly.

"OK, now let's just say that their answer suggested that they were not at all good. Don't tell me what you would say to them in return, but rather, what would you think?"

I considered the political correctness of my answer for a few seconds.

I could reply with the standard feel-good thoughts that most us believe we would have.

That, of course, I would want to ask them if there was anything I could do. No matter the inconvenience to me.

But I opted for honesty; surrendering myself to the lesson that I knew this tale would hold, provided I remained candid and vulnerable.

"I would think that I don't have time for this," I returned with embarrassment.

"Exactly." Douglas broke into a wide, knowing grin. "Brevity due to the busy and hectic nature of our own lives has nothing to do with it. We are simply indifferent as a matter of choice. It's not that we do or don't have time. We simply opt not to make any."

He was making points that I found nearly impossible to counter.

I suppose I had always viewed myself as the charitable sort. The considerate, big-hearted friend and colleague who would do anything for someone in need.

And while my life history had shown that to be mostly true, I began wondering just how much more I could have done.

Should have done.

The perfect spinach suddenly tasted sour in my mouth. But I'm certain it wasn't the leaves' fault. Slight hints of bitterness often accompany emotional uprisings, such as the one I was experiencing, and have a way of making everything taste just a little less crisp.

I turned my focus back to Douglas's words:

"When we pass people and utter simple phrases like 'How are you,' deep down we honestly and truly don't care what the answer is... as long as it doesn't interrupt our day."

The informality of language.

We have become people who ask the questions out of routine and habit, without real regard for the answer.

I was uncomfortable, almost ashamed, in my agreement, but still confused by the practicality.

Of course, the core nature we all share is to both love and be loved unconditionally.

But how?

My brain rifled back through the silent objections I had raised only five minutes before.

Career strain.

Family obligations.

Financial worry.

The never-ending list of "To Dos" we struggle to meet daily.

Are we sincerely present in our interactions with others?

Try as any of us might, how and where do we fit in this type of authenticity when the time constraints and pressures of everyday life seem so frenzied?

Even suffocating.

"The answer," Douglas said, breaking into my thoughts, "is Sawubona."

Part 15

Over the years, I had read countless self-help books in a desperate attempt to find deeper meaning in my life and pinpoint the exact pathway to living in a state of constant happiness.

The promised sanctuary that most of us learn to resent as a mystical land full of prosperity and tranquility, yet impossible to truly find.

Cynically considered a new-age fantasy and adolescent fairy tale by most everyone I knew.

Including myself.

I browsed the Rolodex of my brain, searching for a reference to the word "Sawubona" within the vast collection of self-help resources I had consulted with over the years.

But I was drawing a blank.

"What is Sawubona?" I thought to myself.

"It's a Zulu word that is used to greet someone," Douglas explained, as if again capable of reading my inner dialogue.

"It translates to English as 'I see you.'"

I was intrigued and completely gripped by Douglas's words.

So much so that I barely noticed how my now chilly Atlantic salmon, sitting unfinished in front of me, had become the target for a small group of flies gathering like pestilent children around the tree on Christmas morning.

I slid my plate off to the side, giving the flies their uncontested playground, and leaned forward.

Douglas slanted forward in his own chair to meet me.

"I see you," he repeated.

Part 16

Douglas was speaking with the rapid cadence of an auctioneer.

The emotional and persuasive insistence of a preacher at the climax of his sermon.

He was begging us to hear him.

And if the hairs on the back of my neck, which were now standing at attention and tingling freely in the cool Melbourne breeze, were any indicator, he had found his audience in me.

"When we pass in the streets, I stop. I see you. *All* of you. I look into your eyes, I assess your tone of voice, I find your soul, and I pay attention."

He paused and surveyed the table with a spirited and penetrating scrutiny. His final point was to be the apex.

"Because I truly and authentically care."

Again, I mentally disengaged from the dialogue and began the torturous challenge of examining my own life.

How often I passed others, entombed by my own concerns and entirely unsympathetic to theirs.

How frequently I evoked the customary standard of asking how someone was, without the slightest care for what the answer would be.

How seldom my thoughts or actions were filled by the compassionate desire to serve humankind, rather than consumed by the seduction of realizing my own self-centered quests for success.

"'Sawubona' is used as a formal greeting because human interaction should be formal. It should matter. Just imagine a world where people felt cared for, loved, and supported constantly."

Douglas's words hung perfectly in the frosty night air.

Such simplicity, but so entirely ignored within our hustling world.

Or if not ignored, then inconsistently offered freely.

My head was spinning with visuals from the everyday occurrences we all experience and the nuance of human communication.

How eye contact and a genuine smile can make all the difference when a waitress offers them with her otherwise predictable "hello."

How a casual yet heartfelt touch on the shoulder from a friend reveals his degree of care when listening to your latest setback or most recent heartbreak.

How an honest and telling embrace, along with the words "I love you," ensures that your children don't experience the routine of love, but rather live it as a feeling.

The world could be a different place.

But what I felt in that moment, through Douglas's keen and wise insights, is not what I felt daily.

Very few of us do.

We exist as lifeless shells.

Constantly overwhelmed. Bouncing, without purpose or direction, from one unfulfilling task to the next.

We remain heavy with burden and dark with apathy.

We do not see:

Other people and what they feel.

The world and what it truly offers.

Ourselves and the limitless potential we hold.

That last point — that's the one that, as I sat on the plane, had been haunting me for forty-eight hours.

Is my capacity so much greater than I've ever believed it was?

Is yours?

Part 17

The airplane intercom boomed with the crackle of a message from the flight attendant.

As it jarred me yet again from the immersion of deep reflection, I glanced at my watch and wondered why six announcements within a nine-minute stretch were necessary.

In yet another attempt to get comfortable, I rotated my weary body toward the window on my left and gazed outward.

The engine hum had become more steady and soothing.

The sun was soaking the wing in a dazzling shimmer as it cut easily through the wind with surgical precision.

Far below was a refuge of blue.

The frigid waters of the Pacific appeared still and inviting.

I began to recall more of the treasures Douglas had explained two nights previous.

An intense and clear understanding had started rising within me as I felt my pulse quicken.

"'Sawubona' means to deeply connect. To rejoice in giving all of yourself with each interaction." His playful South African accent still echoed in my brain. "To understand that your purpose in that moment is to see the person in front of you..."

I shot up in my seat with a rapid jolt; my throbbing back and other passengers seated near me objected silently.

A beautiful, thrilling clarity sent me soaring as the most awakened and defining moment of my life took shape at 35,000 feet, somewhere over continental North America.

"Sawubona" is to deeply connect with and see the person in front of you.

But the very essence of the word, the pure and natural doctrine it begs you to live by, must, in every way, be applied to yourself.

You toil through an existence and cling to the self-perceived notions of what you "must" or "should" do, but have you ever truly seen yourself?

Beyond the limits of what society has told you is possible.

Outside the boundaries or what your experiences to date have led you to believe.

Without the definitions or labels of what you have been, done, or achieved so far.

All that we were meant to be and do has been locked away.

Suppressed in the very moments when innocent, childhood imagination gave way to the rules of conformity and acceptability to which we have become slaves.

Happiness and success could not be measured or defined through listing anything tangible, acquiring anything material, nor achieving any societal standard.

I had become hypnotized.

And so have you.

Part 18

If I asked you to tell me who you are, you'd likely start by stating your name.

If I probed you for more information, you'd list off all the things that represent the "you" that you know. You're a mom, a dad, an entrepreneur, an athlete, a psychologist, a cashier, a fitness professional, an internet marketer... The list goes on.

If you felt comfortable and the conversation continued, you might move to secondary classifications such as Christian, Democrat, divorcee, or cancer survivor.

But the truth is, you really aren't any of those things.

Those are labels you wear. Identities that you've become due to the influences and experiences you've have to date. They aren't "good" or "bad," necessarily, but they are most certainly limiting. What's possible for you in life is not a measure of where you've been, but where you decide to go. And that decision often becomes contained to the boundaries of a perforated box, the confines of which you have claimed as the edge of your limits.

The notion reminds me of the very first time I listened to a live lecture on the concepts of Zen.

The Buddhist monk stood with a pitcher of green tea in his hand and a teacup sitting on top of the table in front of him.

Without saying a word, he started pouring.

Nonstop.

Until the cup was completely full and tea started cascading over the sides. He kept pouring—silently—for what seemed like an eternity. Once the pitcher was empty, he placed it beside the cup and spoke very calmly.

"The problem is that most people want to understand Zen as quickly as they can."

It's like he was speaking directly to me.

"But our minds are like a teacup that can no longer receive any more tea. Before we learn what it is, we must first empty our minds of what we believe it to be."

Esoteric? Maybe. But the point the monk made that day has stayed with me ever since. Before you can truly understand your own capacities, you must release yourself from the preconceived definitions of what you think they already are. Before you can embrace who you truly are, you must release yourself from the labels of who you *think* you are.

The greatest revolutions this world has ever known were created by people who had no more luck, intelligence, capacity, or spirit than you.

Which makes you every bit as qualified as anyone else to achieve your dream — no matter what it is. Understand that you don't have to know what you're capable of, just that you are fully capable.

Part 19

When you accept that your life is just a story, it becomes essential to understand what that story is. Where have you drawn the perforated lines of your box? What limits do you place on yourself in all the varying aspects of your life?

This is the essence of "seeing yourself."

The majority of people worldwide who set goals for every facet of their lives do so from the limitations of their self-imposed box. You may feel as though anything is possible, but lack the unconscious belief that it's possible for you. Not because it isn't possible, per se, but simply because you have unknowingly created an identity out of your influences and experiences to date. You aren't aware of how that identity caps or restricts your potential.

The more strongly you identify with a story, the more limiting your capacity becomes to change it and the more it defines your life. But the more awareness you bring to that story, the greater your ability to recognize it as a fluid or flexible perspective, rather than a fixed or rigid border.

I had a client once who felt that everything in her life was a challenge that needed to be overcome. This mindset permeated all parts of her world, from health and fitness to relationships, business, and money.

Her language was a walking testament to her mindset and the lack of awareness she had related to her self-imposed, limiting story. She often spoke about the "difficult" nature of her circumstances and her willingness to rise to the challenge and "beat them" anyway.

In many ways, we mistakenly champion that kind of bravado in our society and define people who use such idioms as "high achievers" or "go-getters." But when your language follows a pattern in which you characterize everything as a challenge, further awareness investigation must be done.

With this particular client, we uncovered an identity she carried for herself that, although superficially motivational, actually served as an incredibly limiting belief in her life on many levels.

She had been born with skeletal abnormalities and underwent several corrective surgeries at a very young age. With every surgery came a battery of physical therapy requirements that would aid in the healing process and ensure that she would have the most normally functioning body possible.

By her early teens, she had risen to each challenge successfully, was enjoying a fully athletic life, and had beaten the odds she had been told were against her from before she could remember.

She had overcome.

But the identity of that label was the seed of many difficulties she faced as an adult.

Due to the influences and experiences of her life to that point, she automatically and unconsciously defined every circumstance and situation as a "challenge." She perceived herself as the overcomer, believed that everything would be a battle, and therefore expected every situation, every circumstance, every goal, and every desire to come replete with struggle.

True to form, her daily actions, habits, and behaviors aligned with that story.

Nothing was easy for her and, although she did experience certain elements of success in many aspects of her life, they were considerably less plentiful than her potential suggested.

Without awareness to our story, we limit our possibilities and make everything much more challenging than it truly is.

Part 20

At the microscopic level, "you" are roughly sixteen trillion electrons.

And electrons don't really have a static definition. They can do pretty much anything. In fact, the only time an electron can be frozen into a definition of what it "is" or "does" is when you observe it.

Now, think about that for a second.

You are nothing more than trillions of electrons. Which means the core of what you are is literally capable of anything. And the only time you ever restrict the weight and incredible power of your capacity is when you "observe" yourself.

When you conclude that what you see as your capacity is somehow an absolute truth. That your beliefs about the supposed limits of your ability are somehow accurate. That your perceptions of your worth are somehow an honest reflection.

Your story of who you believe "you" are is the only thing limiting your potential to do, achieve, create, or become whoever you want.

As a performance coach for the Canadian National Synchronized Skating Team, I helped them qualify for the world championships during an improbable season of success, but I didn't change their on-ice talents...

I changed what they believed was possible.

As a mindset coach working with people worldwide who wanted to do more with their lives, I don't change their goal-setting abilities...

I change the expectations they carried.

As a mentor for gang-affiliated teenagers who want to use music and dance as a way to get themselves off the streets, I don't change their rap skills...

I change their perspective.

Yes, you really can live your dreams and push the boundaries of that perforated box you have called home all these years.

But not before you become aware of the influences and experiences that have created your story and the way they have established limiting thoughts, patterns of language, emotional responses, actions, habits, and behaviors in your everyday life.

We either allow ourselves to evolve or we restrict ourselves from doing so...

SECTION 3: ACCOUNTABILITY

Until you make the unconscious conscious, it will direct your life and you will call it fate.

—C.G. Jung

Part 21

Although this section is not the chronological conclusion, I wrote it last.

I did so because my experiences have shown me that Accountability is the most challenging step in releasing from one's stories, thought patterns, or behavioral styles — which makes tact essential when writing a comprehensive and clear instruction guide about it.

Let me start here:

Accountability does not mean blame.

It does not imply attacking, indicting, or prosecuting oneself, either.

It does not hold harmless the individuals, situations or events that have caused damage, disharmony, or dissension for you in any way.

But it does involve taking co-responsibility for the current state of circumstances in your life.

In short, it may not have been your fault, but it is your problem. And until you decide to take full accountability for the decisions, actions, and reactions you're taking and making in this moment—and moments to come—nothing is ever going to change.

The thing is, you want change.

On some level, we all want change.

And the hardest thing to understand is just how simple change truly is. Simple because it's not something we have to manufacture, create, hustle for, or bring forth. We evolve, naturally and easily, when not being held captive by definitions of truth that we hold as absolute.

Contrary to popular opinion and advice, the first step of allowing change is not to believe you can. The first step is to release yourself from the current belief system you hold. You cannot allow change in your world by artificially implanting a new story of possibility until you take accountability for the fact that the current story you have is just that: a story.

Part 22

We either allow ourselves to evolve and grow or we restrict ourselves from doing so. On both paths, we are guided by an internal mechanism from which all decisions, actions, and reactions are made:

Self-nature.

Our self-nature is split between traits symbolic of light and those typical of darkness. That's not to say that either are good or bad, but for the purposes of your mindset and your accountability over it, they can be separated into serving and non-serving.

Free Nature is serving. From it, liberation is found.

It is joy, bliss, happiness, gratitude, peace, calm, and wakefulness. It is a connection to our own omniscient and omnicompetent capacity. It is our faith that we do not need to know what we're capable of, just that we're fully capable.

While in Free Nature, we are creative; we see solutions without fixating on problems. We experience synchronicity and a deep sense of belief in self, without efforts to manufacture it through affirmations or goals. We do not hinge on the insistence that past events or experiences are accurate predictors of our future. We do not react to people, situations, or circumstances through negativity, spite, frustration, or anger.

We are not removed from our ego, but we no longer operate from it.

Bound Nature is non-serving. In it, we remain enslaved.

It is anger, resentment, greed, envy, comparison, inferiority, cynicism, and fear. It is the cause of over-thinking, self-doubt, procrastination, and all forms of self-sabotage. It is the shadow within which we hide and feel ourselves to be unworthy, broken, and devalued.

While in Bound Nature, we are unproductive, inefficient, victimized, uncertain, and highly reactive. We require external measures of motivation to get us going, only to fall flat when the temporary high wears off. We remain stuck in the purgatory of regretting or resenting the past while stressing or fearing the future.

Our decisions, actions, and reactions stem from ego control.

Part 23

"JUST MAKE THE DECISION TO CHANGE."

That kind of bravado-laden advice seems to be everywhere I turn these days. It's always offered in a provocative, motivational style that's part encouraging, part demeaning.

It seems to embrace the idea that you have the power to change and choose — but if you don't make the decision to do so, you're weak.

Choose to eat better if you're fat.

Choose to be happy if you're sad.

Choose to get over it if you're depressed.

Choose to be wealthy if you're poor.

And, while I don't disagree that everything really is a choice, what we have to either learn or remember is that most people don't REALIZE they have a choice because of a mindset deficit they don't even know exists.

But I'm not handing out Pampers here.

This isn't about advocating for you to stay stuck or to victimize yourself. It is about helping you create SUSTAINABLE change by teaching you the essence of your self-nature and the mechanism by which you can align it to what serves you.

It's not that you can't decide to choose or change, it's that you don't always recognize other decisions or choices that are available to you — no matter how common sense they may appear to others.

Abraham Maslow outlined this brilliantly in his "Stages of Learning" profile.

During the learning process, we ascend through four stages:

- Unconscious Incompetence
- Conscious Incompetence
- Conscious Competence
- Unconscious Competence

For the purpose of explanation, let's use a very basic but very relatable example:

You just got cut off in traffic.

Your immediate reaction is frustration, anger, and annoyance, classic hallmarks of Bound Nature. You express your discontent with a foul face, nasty gesture, and maybe even a choice word to the offender as you reposition yourself on the highway just to give them a piece of your mind — very possibly cutting off someone else to do so.

That's Unconscious Incompetence.

It's a programmed reaction that you've learned to associate with the event of being cut off in traffic. If given the advice to relax and pay no mind to the offense, you'd offer some sort of excuse that it was his fault and you were justified in your response. It's as if you're completely unaware that a different decision or choice was even possible.

Now that I've brought the option of a different outcome to your awareness and asked you to choose otherwise next time, odds are you would ascend into Conscious Incompetence.

This time, at the moment of the offense, you'd remember my advice and know that a different reaction was possible, but you wouldn't have the slightest idea how to choose differently. Frustration, anger, and annoyance would rise up and take over. In a flash, your foul faces, gestures, and language would be dominating the situation once again.

In both cases, Bound Nature would linger and play havoc on your day.

With time and repeated awareness, you'd enter into Conscious Competence and a whole new pattern of reaction.

When cut off, the frustration, anger, and annoyance would begin immediately, but now your awareness of your power to choose would lead to a different outcome. Although agitated in the same way, you could talk yourself down from the explosive temper that once governed your reaction and, through a perspective shift, see clearly just how little foul faces, gestures, and language did anything but rile you up further.

It didn't necessarily feel good on the inside, but your lack of outward reaction means that your ascent into Free Nature has begun. You are learning not just that you have a choice, but also how to assert that choice in the moment.

Continue along that awareness path and you'll land yourself into Unconscious Competence. Quite simply, you could get cut off in traffic twice in the same morning without as much as a twinge of emotion. Your former eruptions into Bound Nature are distant memories of the old you.

Yes, you can "JUST MAKE THE DECISION TO CHANGE."

But not without first accepting that the way you see the world is just a matter of your current perspective, growing aware of what that perspective is and that you have a choice in it, and, finally, taking accountability for the fact that your perspective is not absolutely true and that you are not a victim of it.

Part 24

One of the most important ways of learning the difference between Bound Nature and Free Nature is to appreciate how they affect us. Maslow's Stages of Learning apply here as well.

At first, we don't know what Bound Nature is or the impact it has on us.

Once we gain some awareness, we know when we're in Bound Nature, but feel powerless against it.

With further awareness, we experience the impact of Bound Nature, but no longer react from it or allow it to linger.

Eventually, we don't live much of our lives in Bound Nature at all.

In order to help my clients and students gain as much awareness as possible, so that they can be as accountable as possible, I help them understand the four ways through which Bound Nature presents itself:

1. Thoughts
2. Feelings
3. Behaviors
4. Physical symptoms

Negative self-talk is very common in our society and something most people can relate to. When our inner dialogue is harsh, demeaning, frustrated, angry, over-chattering, cynical, envious, or critical, we are in Bound Nature.

Heavy, dark emotions are another shared experience that many know well. When we feel sad, empty, agitated, anxious, afraid, or demoralized, we are in Bound Nature.

Holding habits or behaviors that do not align with our goals is an additional reference point to which most people relate. When we procrastinate, avoid, waste time aimlessly, or live in a constantly inefficient state, we are in Bound Nature.

Finally, general aches, as well as specific pain points that do not originate from a particular injury or illness, can very much be associated with Bound Nature. Anxiety is often carried in the chest, worry in the neck and shoulders, and guilt in the lower back.

We can travel a lifetime without being aware of the incessant negative talk in our mind, the heavy burden of emotion in our heart, the lethargy in our actions, and the prevailing pain in our body that we simply come to think of as "normal."

In understanding Bound Nature and Free Nature, the first order of accountability is simply recognizing which of these two states of your self-nature you are in at any given moment in time.

Part 25

If you were to stand in the middle of a merry-go-round, your choice of reaction or response would be limited to one of two.

Either keep your gaze forward and calmly stare to the horizon as the mechanical horses blur around you, or notice each and every horse as it passes, eventually becoming transfixed on one until you begin turning in circles uncontrollably.

Those mechanical horses are the metaphorical equivalent of your negative past experiences, current stresses, toxic people in your life, or any other form of trigger that takes you to a non-serving place. You cannot always prevent them from circling around you endlessly. But you have a choice over whether they force you to stare at, direct your energy toward, or otherwise connect with them as they spin you into a dizzy mess.

That is the measure of true accountability.

There is no past life experience that forces you to act or react a certain way. Not without your permission to allow it to do so.

There is no current stress, toxic person, or incidental trigger that compels you to respond or behave a certain way. Not without you granting approval for things to transpire in such a manner.

Accountability is where release from fear, self-doubt, and limitation begins. It is an acknowledgment that however tragic, stressful, emotional, or negatively inciting any event or person is, our reactions to them are ours and ours alone. When we blame, we effectively deny the power we have to shape the life we want and, in the process, keep ourselves enslaved to a repetitive, harmful cycle that ensures we will never find true happiness, self-love, or success.

Once we are equipped with the knowledge that we have a choice and empowered by the awareness that allows us to make that choice, we can begin to observe our Bound Nature rather than experience it.

To experience is to react. When we experience, we allow the negative thoughts, emotional memories, or adverse situations into us and give them control. It is the essence of being led by the mechanical horses into a bewildering spin through which we lose perspective on ourselves, our footing, our peace, and our freedom.

In contrast, to observe is the art of non-reaction. When we observe, we accept that negative thoughts, emotional memories, or adverse situations sometimes swirl around us, without letting them own the moment. It is the Free Nature state of maintaining our liberty no matter the temperament, speed, or volume of those mechanical horses.

It's worth noting that perfection does not exist.

Understanding Bound Nature, Free Nature, and the dance of accountability is a constant but gentle journey. Challenging days happen. Difficult moments exist. Demanding and confrontational people rear their heads. Sometimes we will react. Sometimes we will experience rather than observe.

There is no error in that. No need for self-criticizing or concluding that you are broken. The truth is, I firmly believe that every human being alive has the power and ability to deliver themselves from the fears, self-doubts, and limitations that keep them bound. All that's needed is the right environment and tools that allow the process to happen naturally.

Accountability is the foundation of passive adaptation.

Without so much as trying to create change, you will begin to shift your perspective completely. You will begin to see yourself, the world, your opportunities, and your potential from an entirely different viewpoint.

What was once considered impossible for you will no longer carry that definition.

You will have cultivated and nourished the soil of your mindset.

And from there, you can now actively plant the seeds you choose to blossom...

Your mindset is the handbrake. If it's
locked, you go nowhere...

SECTION 4: ADAPTATION

*Those who cannot change their minds
cannot change anything.*

—George Bernard Shaw

Part 26

You're standing at the bottom of what feels like a very deep hole.

The walls seem impossible to climb, but that doesn't stop you from trying to claw your way out. Some days, you manage to make headway and can feel the warm glow of the sun of your face. Most days, though, it doesn't seem to matter how hard you pull, struggle, or battle. I suppose it's actually fair to say that, as your intensity of effort increases, so too does the feeling of hopelessness.

Life wasn't supposed to be like this.

Spent at the bottom of a hole.

The blue sky, inviting breeze, and clear, unclouded views are all within reach. But you just can't ever get close enough to them for any length of time. Every time you start to climb your way out, another setback sends you spiraling downward; either a new blow that you weren't expecting or an old story that you can't ever seem to outrun.

A motivational guru walks by and you can't help but call out in desperation.

"Hey you! You up there walking by. I'm stuck in this hole, could you please help me?"

The motivational guru smiles wide and begins his sermon.

He talks about the great men and women of history who have overcome impossible circumstances. His voice booms with enthusiasm and his cadence sends a vibrant energy that you can feel even from the bottom of your hole. He tells you that winners will never quit and that only the weak surrender. Even in this somewhat hopeless state, you can't help but get excited. You feel inspired to act and determined to climb your way out this time.

As his lecture ends, the motivational guru walks on.

Still exhilarated, you begin to heave, tug, and jerk at the slippery walls of your hole. Fatigue sets in, but you refuse to surrender. Only quitters and the weak surrender. You remember the motivational guru's words and his examples of those esteemed men and women of yesteryear who overcame more than just a basic hole.

So you pull.

Force.

Drive, push, hoist, and drag.

But nothing seems to work. Not sustainably.

For every inch you gained, you ended up losing three.

You try with everything you have to recreate the intensity, confidence, and inspiration you felt while the motivational guru was talking, but you just can't seem to summon the emotion.

The positivity and courage you felt not more than a few hours ago have been replaced by cold, isolating pangs that you know very well, because you've felt them before.

Helpless and demoralized.

You don't mean to feel self-pity and always end up wearing the burden of guilt when you do. You understand that there are many people in the world who exist in holes much deeper and bleaker than your own and that all you're supposed to need is inspiration, gratitude, and action.

Be inspired to create an extraordinary life, they say.

Feel grateful for what you have, they tell you.

Just take action on what you want, they explain.

It's not that you disagree with any of that, but you've tried. You've tried and it never seems to work.

Just then, a success expert strolls past, so you call up in desperation again.

"Hey you! You up there walking by. I'm stuck in this hole, could you please help me?"

The success expert exudes confidence and begins her lesson.

She talks about the strategic plans you need for getting out of the hole. Her demeanor is self-assured, almost fearless in nature, and she teaches you how to better leverage your time and systems in order to gain an improved return on investment for your climbing efforts. Even from the bottom of your hole, a sense of optimism starts creeping in. The success expert's blueprint for success seems to have worked for her and all the other case studies of people she told you about. Intoxicated by the potential, you're ready to give it another shot.

As her instruction ends, the success expert walks on.

You begin to apply the strategy. You plan your approach, formulate your game plan, and take action with great energy. Confusion and doubt lurk non-stop, but you know that you need to keep hustling.

So you grind it out, day after day.

Press on no matter what.

Go, go, go and then go some more.

But nothing seems to work. Not sustainably.

For every inch you gained, you ended up losing three.

Part 27

No matter what you may believe at this present moment, "the hole" is not an uncommon place for anyone walking the planet. Some holes are deeper, some seem bottomless; some are temporary and some more everlasting and suffocating.

But you can rest assured that absolutely no one can claim immunity from, or lack of familiarity with, the hole. I have worked with extremely successful businessmen who lost the poise and self-reliance that created their successes to begin with. World-class athletes who experienced lapses in morale or unexpected crises of confidence that dramatically affected their performance. Even couples who lost touch with the simplicity and mutual respect their relationships were built on.

Whether it encompasses your entire life or simply a facet of it, this circumstance can infiltrate your mental and emotional well-being. What I hope to have illustrated with my parable above is that *you* are the co-conspirator of getting yourself into the hole and, therefore, the primary catalyst for getting yourself out.

The very reason that most motivational, success-directed, or even spiritual solutions have proven partially or completely ineffective for you is that they often bypass the foundational steps on which a journey must be based. Either they bypass them in the hope of selling you a "quick-fix," or you decide to ignore the scope of their advice in your haste to create immediate change for the better.

But "journey" doesn't have to imply "lengthy," and immediate change is not at all impossible or absurd — provided we stop looking outside ourselves with questions whose answers will be found within.

Before we can heed the recommendation to change the perspective we hold about ourselves, we must first ACCEPT that our perspective is fluid and not at all absolute.

Before we can apply the suggestion to simply change our thoughts, we must first become AWARE of what our thoughts are and how they create limits and barriers.

Before we can act on the advice to change our actions and behaviors every day, we must first take ACCOUNTABILITY for our part in creating them.

The motivational gurus and success experts aren't wrong.

The dream you carry for your life is the fuel.

And your actions, the vehicle.

But your mindset is the handbrake. If it's locked, you go nowhere. When it's released, you will go anywhere you want.

Rather than expending all your efforts on creating goals to pursue, or bathing in rhetoric designed to make you pursue them faster, spend time truly embracing that your life is just a story. Once you become both mindful of the current narrative and conscious that the pen is squarely in your hand to write whatever you like, you will become fully empowered to twist the plot at any moment towards the next chapter of your choice.

That's the merit and magic of passive adaptation.

When you shift your perspective from rigid and permanent to dynamic and mobile, everything begins to change. You literally start seeing the world through different eyes and begin experiencing a new sense of possibility where only impossibility existed before.

Part 28

My dad used to tell me this story about a small stretch of land that would never grow anything successfully.

As a teenager living on a farm in rural Italy, he and my grandfather would set goals every year about what they wanted to plant on that particular section of their property.

My dad would work his butt off.

He would evoke willpower, hustle, and all the conventional advice that you receive when seeking information on how to turn your dreams into reality.

But it never mattered.

Nothing ever grew.

Years later, my dad came to discover that under the few feet of topsoil was a layer of pure rock.

This completely explained why nothing ever blossomed no matter how many goals he set, how hard he worked, or how much willpower he demonstrated.

The solution to success is seldom about the need to set better goals, work harder, or show more willpower — no matter what your objective.

It's about your mindset.

The hidden layer underneath that topsoil.

Change that and success grows like a weed.

Don't change that, and no amount of hard work or willpower will ever be enough.

Whether your goals are based on weight loss, business, money, happiness, or love, the path to realization is about nourishing the soil of your mindset. You do this by accepting that your past experiences are merely perspectives, becoming acquainted with the perspectives you currently carry, and taking responsibility over the power you have to change those perspectives.

No matter how perfect the seed you plant, its eventual success or failure is based solely on whether or not the soil is prepared to foster its growth.

The world is full of people living at the bottom of a lonely, frustrating hole. They have sought out help and direction from capable fitness experts, business coaches, and money mentors only to find themselves in the same plight of one step forward, three steps back — even after investing time and energy into the offered solution.

In most cases, the seeds given by the experts, coaches, and mentors are well crafted and contain vast potential for growth. But in the presence of an unhealthy soil that is bound by fear, limitation, or doubt, even the most perfect seed won't blossom.

It's one thing to say "no fear," but quite another to actually silence the fears that keep you stuck and uncertain. It's rather simple to call yourself "limitless," but very challenging to release from the limitations that maintain borders around you. It might be easy to claim "unshakable confidence," but much harder to purge the doubts that stop you from taking action on your dreams.

When it comes to achieving anything you want in life, the health of your soil is much more important than the perfection of your seed. Through Acceptance, Awareness, and Accountability, we gain the freedom of choosing our perspective. In doing so, we experience a passive adaptation to our mindset (the soil) for the better.

Seeds will begin budding with more ease and less complication.

Self-worth will increase as fears, limitations, and doubts begin to wane in intensity, frequency, and power.

That said, the true, lasting achievement of your goals will occur when you create and implement a practical plan for success and happiness that will free you from the things that continue to hold you back.

I must caution:

Active adaptation of your mindset can't be an occasional longing.

It's an everyday effort.

Fortunately, the 60-Minute Mindset is designed to make daily application very simple.

Part 29

The following parts of this book contain the methods for actively creating a success-driven, happy mindset that will allow you to achieve all the goals and intentions you have for life while enabling you to enjoy peace, balance, and contentment.

This method—which I call the 6-Pack or 60-Minute Mindset—is a series of six separate exercises that form an interdependent system and take you roughly one hour per day to execute.

It is very important to recognize that the 6-Pack does not replace your need to take action on your goals or intentions. This is not a quasi-spiritual invitation to enlist no effort or partial labor in the hopes that merely thinking your desires into reality has any chance of being successful.

The experts and gurus can teach you how to set goals, make money, lose weight, enhance your business, or incorporate strategies. Those are the familiar seeds that millions of people across the world look to plant every single day.

The 6-Pack is your method for cultivating the soil. It will make your actions more directed, your work more effortless, your effectiveness more profound, and your results more predictable.

But in truth, I'm undercutting it completely.

Through the incorporation of a 6-Pack into people's daily habits, I have witnessed successes of dramatic proportions, from sports and business endeavors to cases of depression and relationship reconciliations.

I have worked with children as young as eleven and adults as old as sixty-five.

From people who were already wildly successful and wanted to push their boundaries to the next level to those who had been trying but failing virtually their entire lives.

Many of my clients had spent thousands of dollars on "seed" information prior to coming to me, yet their results were often negligible. The instruction they received was not faulty or inadequate, but as your mindset goes, so goes your success potential. They had been planting high-quality seeds in a soil of mud and garnering the penalties of doing so.

They were equipped with all the knowledge for *what* to do to achieve their goals, as well as the process for *how* to do it. But inaction continued. Doubt persisted. Fear intensified. Their limitations of what they believed possible narrowed even further.

The 6-Pack is a method for expansion.

It expands your perspective beyond what you believe to be possible right now.

It expands your self-worth, which mutes doubt.

It expands confidence by quieting fear.

It pushes the boundaries of your self-imposed, perforated box beyond your wildest dreams.

The individual components of the 6-Pack are:

(1) Imagination Theater

(2) Silence

(3) Intention Review

(4) Recognition & Appreciation

(5) Next Day Preparation

(6) Triggers

Why are they effective and necessary?

How are they interdependently important?

When do you execute them each day?

Let us begin...

Part 30

1. Imagination Theater

What It Is

I first saw the practical application of this technique while working as a performance coach for the Canadian National Synchronized Skating Team in 1998.

Right from the beginning of the season, before the choreography for their intricate on-ice performances had even been fully developed, skaters would engage in a daily visualization routine.

They would see themselves skating flawlessly, as if from the vantage point of a fan watching from the stands. They would imagine watching themselves executing a perfect routine with their own eyes and incorporate intentional physical movements—such as artistic arm positions or facial expressions—into the technique to make the experience more real and life-like.

It's important to note that, at the beginning of a season, before any specifics had been created relating to music selection or even what competitions they would attend during the year, the Imagination Theater technique could only be used as a broad exercise. No details were available for the skaters to paint a specific image, but that was hardly a deterrent.

Instead, they practiced the skill of Imagination Theater using mental images, emotions, and sensations from past experiences in their skating careers. Over time, as the year progressed, we layered new imagery into the exercise to enhance the specificity.

As musical pieces for the routines were finalized, they would play over the speakers during the Imagination Theater portion of our practices. As our competitive schedule became clearer, we'd try to locate photographs of the arenas we'd be visiting so the exact images of the ice surface, stands, backdrops, and colors could be incorporated into the technique.

I've found that to be a critically important progression for people to understand.

Many times I have been told, while teaching this particular technique, that a sense of intimidation or fear wells up because people often don't know exactly what to envision. Meaning that they don't have any specific goals or frames of reference to know what success will look and feel like.

The goal of Imagination Theater is to simply get started, grow in proficiency, and make it a habitual part of your day. If you lack a specific goal or seem to struggle with making the exercise of visualization as specific as it needs to be in order to be effective, just remember my example of the National Team athletes I used to work with.

With them, a specific goal or vision was a virtual impossibility at the beginning of a season, so we merely turned our attention to making it a more general exercise at first by focusing on a "familiar location" rather than "exact address." What started as a somewhat vague visualization exercise in locker rooms and arenas throughout North America became highly specific and precise in the European equivalents as our season marched toward international competitions and the world championships.

Everyone has a sense of the direction they want their lives to travel, a hunch or hint of what it is they want to achieve, obtain, become, or do. So use that as your backdrop. In the absence of having a clear, definite purpose or "exact address," simply begin to rehearse your life as you want to see it by taking yourself to a general vision or "familiar location" from your built-in sense of direction.

How To Do It

For 15-30 minutes every day, I want you to sit in a chair, lie on your bed, or just get comfortable in any position that best suits you.

For the experience to be maximized, I suggest that you enjoy your Imagination Theater in relative or complete silence or, even better, while listening to soft, soothing music.

Once comfortable, close your eyes and begin to imagine.

Paint rich, vivid mental images that illustrate you achieving, obtaining, becoming, or doing what you most want in life. Bring as much detail to the scenery as possible. From sounds and smells to emotion, locations, situations, and people. The more real you make this experience, the greater the impact.

As your mind wanders away from the image you're building—and it will—bring it back into focus calmly, without growing frustrated or becoming obsessive. Imagination Theater is a practiced art and you will gain skill and ability over time and through concerted effort.

In order to learn how to perform Imagination Theater effectively, I've created a twenty-minute audio program for you called "Changing the Story."

It will guide you through the process of Imagination Theater and allow you to stay focused on creating the vision you want.

Please enjoy that audio through the following website:

www.MyMindsetTools.com

Why To Do It

The image we hold in our conscious thoughts and surround with powerful emotions is what our life becomes.

But that's not nearly as mystic, supernatural, or occult-like as it may sound.

Mental imagery has been part of the ascension towards success for every athlete I've ever worked with. It is taken every bit as seriously as their physical training or injury rehabilitation.

Not only does this exercise provoke immense amounts of certainty, confidence, and belief in your ability to achieve what you want, it will also begin impacting the decisions you make, actions you take, and behaviors you execute on a daily basis.

If repeated in faith and with expectancy, your unconscious mind—which has no capacity to discern thoughts, emotions, or images as real versus imagined—will simply accept this version of your life as reality. You become your own day-to-day influence and start changing the story housed in the unconscious mind. In turn, the unconscious mind will begin directing your emotional responses, actions, behaviors, and habits toward the images you feed it.

The truth is that you already use Imagination Theater every single day without realizing it.

Whatever influences and experiences you've had to date, they have created perceptions, belief systems, and expectations that live in the unconscious and account for your self-talk and actions—or inactions—on a daily basis. If you want but lack anything in your life, you can bet that the repeated images, words, and emotions playing on repeat in your unconscious mind are the reason why.

Imagination Theater is where you can learn to use your imagination for you, rather than against you.

When To Do It

Perform Imagination Theater every morning for 15-30 minutes.

And once again, please enjoy "Changing the Story" through this website:

www.MyMindsetTools.com

Part 31

2. Silence

What It Is

I learned the incredible value of silence—or meditation—very early in life from one of the most esteemed teachers in the world.

At the age of seventeen and after many months of confusing, seemingly unconnected symptoms, I was diagnosed as having a chronic stress disorder. Fortunately for me, my physician had no interest in prescribing medication or suggesting that I seek the support of a counselor.

Instead, he gave me the brochure to a clinic in downtown Toronto, where I lived, called the Relaxation Response Institute. That's where I met Eli Bay.

It was 1991, but Eli had been teaching the techniques and explaining the benefits of meditation to individuals and corporations throughout Canada and the United States for many years already. He is considered a pioneer in bringing the practical application of meditation and stress-relief methods to contemporary North America and was doing so long before they became trendy.

Every week, I sat in Eli's workshops at the institute, completely fascinated. The only teenager in his study groups, I listened with intent to his lectures about Buddhist philosophy, theories of quantum mechanics, universal laws, elements of spirituality, and how they all applied to real life in a real world.

Through Eli's programs, other formal education, and several years of self- exploration, I was exposed to and have practiced various forms of silence, including transcendental, walking, guided, and autogenic. My life was changed by these experiences and, to this day, I participate in some form of silence or meditative technique daily.

I must share an important word to the wise, however.

The degree to which meditation has become popular—even fashionable—in our current culture doesn't come without concerns. In my wildest imagination, and even after twenty years of immersive practice, I would never consider touting myself as any sort of meditation expert or enlightened sage on the topic.

Taking any number of minutes in a day to simple relax and be without thought is good. It's better than good.

But Dr. Robert Masters coined a term called "Spiritual Bypassing" that I feel is worth a mention here. Among other facets, the concept of Spiritual Bypassing speaks to those who "do" an activity without actually doing it. It's not the least bit challenging to lie down or sit cross-legged in front of a fire while projecting a calm facade, but not actually engage in a meditative state — even though you might portray yourself as someone deeply connected or spiritually wise.

True silence is about remaining conscious, focused, and yet empty of thought all at the same time. It takes practice and patience, but it is more than worth the journey.

My other word of caution applies if you are at all averse to this idea.

Let me take a moment to assure you that my brand of silence is not about third-eye acuity, being guided by spirits long since dead, or elevating your body and defying gravity in the process.

Quite the opposite.

I believe in guided forms of silence because they are much more simple, reasonable, and enjoyable in the beginning of your journey. Even for more advanced people, I still prefer to use guided silence tracks that are created with advancement in mind.

How To Do It

For 15-30 minutes every day, I want you to sit in a chair, lie on your bed, or just get comfortable in any position that best suits you, just as you did with Imagination Theater.

The general idea with silence is to keep your conscious attention directed towards, and in contact with, a very specific anchor or focal point while allowing your mind to empty all other aspects of thought.

The cadence of your breath is widely taught as an ideal focal point.

There is a natural, hypnotic rhythm within the inhalation-exhalation sequence of your breathing that soothes and provides a logical, almost instinctive focal point for your directed concentration. Focusing on specific areas of your body, colors, or even words can also work as awareness points.

Silence truly is a gift to the mind, body, and soul once performed with regularity. The benefits are vast and immediate, but please understand that learning to quiet your mind is among the most challenging things you could ever embark upon. Far too many people give up on practicing silence daily because of these challenges.

In order to help my own clients worldwide establish daily silence habits through a guided, supported system, I created a program called "The Art of Silence," which I would like you to have for no cost.

It contains three separate audio tracks that guide you into a blissful state of silence and allow for maximum benefit for beginner, intermediate, and advanced practitioners of silence. I've also built a daily tracker in which you can record your silence experiences and create a self-customized lifelong habit.

Please enjoy "The Art of Silence" through this website:

www.MyMindsetTools.com

The audio tracks and daily tracker are available for immediate access.

Why To Do It

The benefits of engaging in regular silence are both tremendous and well-documented.

In my own experiences, I have seen silence aid in stress reduction, injury rehabilitation, illness healing, improved athletic performance, and increased business productivity. As a natural consequence of living in the world we do, our bodies tend to exist in the sympathetic range of our nervous system on a regular basis. This is the "fight or flight" response that is organic within the human construct and quite necessary for survival from a biological standpoint.

But it is not a state we were meant to remain in for long periods of time, and it can create disastrous effects related to physical health as well as emotional and mental well-being. Silence triggers the parasympathetic segment of our nervous systems, which serves to calm, de-stress, and relax us systemically. It is from this peaceful state that we are able to restore, renew, and repair.

From a strictly mindset-related perspective, silence is a catalyst for creativity and focus.

Learning to minimize conscious brain chatter is a powerful method for tapping into solution centers within our mind that become largely muted by the never-ending barrage of thinking we do on a daily basis. It is positively astounding to realize that the answers to our questions and clarity on our confusion truly are within us. Rather than continually looking outside ourselves for the solutions we crave, it is both empowering and inspiring to enlist a habit that frees us from fears, self-doubts, and limitations that make us believe we are not capable.

When To Do It

Experience silence every evening for 15-30 minutes.

And once again, please enjoy "The Art of Silence" through this website:

www.MyMindsetTools.com

Part 32

3. Intention Review

What It Is

As odd as it may seem, Intention Review became a mainstay in my life during college when I worked as a bouncer and bodyguard on the weekends.

From nine p.m. to three a.m. every Thursday, Friday, and Saturday evening, my life involved the loud, drama-oriented, and sometimes violent setting associated with bars, nightclubs, and concerts. My weekends featured music pumping so loudly that I could still feel it inside my body for hours after leaving an event, constant haggling with drunken patrons, and inevitable fights that required me to either break up attacks or defend myself from them.

As a young man, I certainly didn't mind the job or the atmosphere I found myself in every weekend. But I was dedicated to my studies and began to notice how much separation I felt between myself and my course work come Sunday afternoon. I had to re-motivate myself to get to the assignments or studying that was required for the coming week, but not just because of the natural fatigue I experienced after three consecutive late nights.

It was more of a visceral disconnect.

In college, I had clearly defined goals and specific intentions for what I wanted to accomplish, both in the immediate aspect of a given test, assignment, or exam as well as my long-term vision of where my education would lead me career-wise.

But every weekend, those clear definitions and specific intentions would be completely suspended. Entirely forgotten. As if my college world no longer existed and the objectives I carried for my life no longer mattered. Getting myself motivated on Sunday afternoon wasn't about overcoming fatigue or conquering any sort of laziness. It was the action of having to reconnect with my direction in life and being inspired to stay on that path.

I created a system for myself that involved intentionally reviewing both my immediate workload for the coming week's classes as well as the longer-range target of my career at large. I would spend 10-15 minutes every single time I came home from a bar, club, or concert simply reviewing notes, reading over assignments, and mentally rehearsing my goals.

As small a gesture as this may seem, it proved incredibly powerful. I learned the art of staying connected to my immediate and future goals, which gave me the ability to fashion an ethos, or governing philosophy, for my life and its direction, no matter what variables, intangibles, circumstances, or situations may arise.

Intention Review is precisely that.

Deliberately examining and affirming the clearly defined goals and specific intentions you have for your life: a given project, business venture, athletic target, or any other objective you have in your sightlines for achievement.

How To Do It

The first step is to write a Specificity of Intention. I will outline a strategy for this in detail in Section 5 of this book.

Once you have established your Specificity of Intention, it is imperative to write it in the back of your Recognition Journal, which I will explain in the following 6-Pack segment. Write it out in its long form without abbreviations or shortcuts and in the absence of unneeded explanations, descriptions, or narratives. This is a simple and powerful statement related to what it is you choose to create, achieve, do, or become.

Once per day—preferably at the same time each day—you will focus all of your conscious attention on this statement while reading it aloud or quietly in your head. Read it several times while listening to instrumental music that inspires you.

It is critical that you bring all of your attention to the words and don't merely read with partial effort or while distracted. Moreover, when constructing your Specificity of Intention, I advise that you create a strong visual and emotional connection to the words. When reading and re-reading your statement daily, bring life, feeling, and imagination to the experience. The words should not simply be read, but felt through the vision and emotion they carry.

Read, visualize, and bring emotion to your Specificity of Intention for 5-10 minutes.

With my own clients, I teach both this version of Intention Review as well as other forms that involve poetic rhythm and strategies for crafting statements that bypass the objections that can often come from our conscious brain. In order to have your Specificity of Intention flow directly into your unconscious and become the new language of your mindset, creating shorter, emotive versions that you can listen to throughout the day is extremely powerful.

I have produced a short tutorial for you on how to create and incorporate your own Intention Review system into your day, as well as the variations I teach to my personal clients worldwide.

Please enjoy that tutorial and the associated tools I've built for you through this website:

www.MyMindsetTools.com

The tutorial and tools are available for immediate access.

Why To Do It

Each day of your life presents wins and losses, triumphs and struggles, successes and defeats, but no matter how much the motivational zealots tell you to hustle your way through it or to remember that within every challenge lies a lesson from which you can get better, the accumulated weight of a constantly shifting pendulum can wear heavy on even the most inspired soul.

Building a success-driven mindset really isn't about pretending the ups and downs of life don't exist or acting as though they don't impact you. It isn't about fluctuating in mood or ambition due to the external circumstances surrounding you or attaching your sails to the direction of life events as they transpire around you, either.

It's about maintaining a course and direction no matter the condition of the seas you're in.

This is a daily system that serves as your compass and keeps the specificity of your intention at the top of your mind, always. When done routinely, your Intention Review makes where you're going much more certain and assured, while making where you are feel significantly less permanent. It helps override any conscious thoughts related to scarcity, lack of belief, or confusion that you may experience on any given day and ensures that the powerful inner dialogue of your unconscious shifts permanently in your favor, rather than remaining in opposition.

When To Do It

Perform your Intention Review as one of the last things you do every evening before going to bed.

And once again, please enjoy the tutorial and tools I have for you through this website:

www.MyMindsetTools.com

Part 33

4. Recognition & Appreciation

What It Is

In my days as a performance coach for world-class athletes at the Olympic, professional, and national team level, I became intimately aware of one of the most striking features that separated the truly successful from those who continually struggled.

Mindset at large was the primary factor; more succinctly, the habit of frequently recognizing and praising their own efforts.

I know it's customary to believe that elite athletes are all very hard-driving, headstrong, self-deprecating individuals who are forever angry at themselves for poor performances or frustrated with their own efforts, but my experiences show the opposite to be true.

The best of the best that I ever had the honor of working with had exceptional capacities of perspective that enabled them to maintain high levels of consistency while remaining very simplistic in their approach to daily priorities.

In fact, it is from working with high-end athletes that I generated the life ethos "Simplicity + Consistency = Success."

Developing frustration due to a poor performance, either in the training room or during competition, serves only to create a disgruntled outlook that will certainly carry into tomorrow. When million-dollar contracts or inclusion on national teams is at stake, that kind of attitude is completely undesirable.

The action of Recognition & Appreciation is intended to purposefully observe and note the quality efforts you put forth toward your goals every day — no matter how seemingly insignificant they may appear to be. It also involves showing appreciation to the people who played a role in your directed efforts that day.

How To Do It

I have each of my own clients purchase a Recognition Journal at the beginning of their work with me. The purpose of this journal is to record the daily progress they make towards their Specificity of Intention.

On even the most challenging, stress-filled, or unproductive days, there are always small victories or essential steps you take, no matter how nominal they may be.

The directive is to review your day from the moment you awoke and carefully consider everything you did that brought you closer to your objectives. *Everything* you did. The unfortunate condition of our society is that we only ever seem to rejoice in the large achievements or notable accomplishments of our efforts. But not only does that keep us constantly and unrealistically striving to crack a home run on a daily basis, it stops us from seeing the vital singles we end up hitting each and every day.

Recognize three things you did each day that were in concert with the goals you are in the process of achieving. Then consider three people who were either instrumental or influential in helping you pursue those goals. Be sure to reach out toward each of those three people in that moment, thanking them for their impact and shipping them some gratitude.

I refer to this exercise as "Me 3 + Ship 3."

I've prepared a lesson and template that illustrates how to create your own Recognition Journal and use it on a daily basis.

Please enjoy that lesson and the template through this website:

www.MyMindsetTools.com

The lesson and template are available for immediate access.

Why To Do It

Whether you know it or not, or like it or not, your unconscious mind will dwell through the night on the last conscious thoughts you give it before falling asleep.

If you are annoyed, frustrated, angry, dejected, or unnerved by your efforts and performance from the day, or feeling hopeless and dreading tomorrow, those are the exact thoughts and emotions you will awake with. Instead, purposefully nourish your mind by recognizing your achievements of the day and being grateful for those who contributed, especially in the context of your goal and how much those achievements brought you one step closer to it. This "mind nourishment" will flood into your unconscious and create a dualistic sense of excitement at the prospect of your goal achievement and peace in the journey you are on to do so.

Secondarily, but no less significantly, the action of praising yourself and thanking others simply feels good. Whether we view that in the spiritual realm or mental dimension, it flows into our physical presence; feeling good in body, mind, and soul matters both in life satisfaction and in remaining confident in your ability to achieve.

When To Do It

Perform your Recognition & Appreciation as one of the last things you do every evening before going to bed.

And once again, please enjoy the lesson and tutorial I have for you through this website:

www.MyMindsetTools.com

Part 34

5. Next Day Preparation

What It Is

Whether we're talking about athletic victory, business ascension, or personal achievement, I have never witnessed anyone succeed if preparation isn't the cornerstone of their values. I'll go as far as saying—no matter how contentious or foreign a claim it is to many people—that in the pursuit of success, roughly eighty percent of your time should be spent on preparation and the remaining twenty percent allocated to executing the tasks needed to take you there.

Simply put, preparing to succeed is what makes success possible.

When I consider the flow and structure of my own daily schedule, it is deeply invested in mindful, deliberate efforts toward planning my path and establishing a mindset that will help me actualize my goals, while limiting actual tasks to a few specific, high-priority items that I attack with purpose and optimal focus.

The same is true for every high achiever I have ever known and precisely what I teach to my own personal clients.

Next Day Preparation is an activity in which you list out the order of your actions for tomorrow and mindfully prepare for their achievement. It is not obsessive, not a doctrine that you should consider cast in stone or unshakable. Without question, over-fixating on an exactness of how tomorrow will go can lead to strain and annoyance if life circumstances flow in opposition to your plan. Having a dynamic, go-with-the-flow mentality is a key component of enjoying the fruits of a success-driven, happy mindset, but that should never be confused with someone who is content to play at the whims of life.

Freedom is gained when we release ourselves from the compulsion to try to control every aspect of our world, but allow for maximal creativity and fulfillment by structuring the parts that we can.

How To Do It

Use whatever mode and method you choose with respect to planning and organizing your daily schedule. Personally—and after years of experimentation—I have found myself right back where I started two decades ago: with a pen and piece of paper.

For each month of a six- or twelve-month cycle, create a descending list of items as follows: Outcome, Intention, and Action Steps.

The Outcome is the goal in written form. Where you intend to be or what you intend to have achieved by the end of this month.

The Intention is a master list of items that you either know or can speculate must be done in order to meet that Outcome.

The Action Steps are a subset of actionable items that all need to be done to reach the Outcome.

One of the most important reasons for categorizing your goals in this sequence is the immense confusion and overwhelming emotion that most people feel immediately upon setting their sights on achieving something significant. By stating clearly where you're going and then establishing a plan to get there, you not only improve your chances of success dramatically, you prevent many of the things that often derail people from pursuing their goals such as overthinking, uncertainty, and emotional paralysis.

Next Day Preparation is the simple exercise of extracting the most pressing or logical items from your Action Steps list and ordering them in sequence to be executed the following day.

I have prepared a lesson that helps you understand how Next Day Preparation works within the structure of a monthly goals system, as well as the method through which you can create monthly systems of your own.

Please enjoy that resource here:

www.MyMindsetTools.com

It is available for immediate access.

Why To Do It

There are many advantages to performing Next Day Preparation regularly, but from a mindset perspective, one of the most important is peace.

Very often, people's days are filled with commotion, distraction, and time constraints that make them feel life will always be experienced at breakneck speeds and with unpredictable chaos. Not only is this a highly incorrect perspective to carry, it makes successfully achieving a goal feel almost impossible and leaves the impression that we have no control in the matter.

Next Day Preparation gives us the ability to be proactive in creating the twenty-four hours we want, rather than reacting to those we're given. We can establish peace of mind by simply refusing to dance with the disorganization and instead de-clutter our mental chatter from the events of the past day or negative outlooks for tomorrow.

Secondarily, but no less significantly, Next Day Preparation provides an innate checks and balances system from which you can monitor your efficiency. No matter your goal or intention, the need to be effective, not busy, with your efforts is essential. Busyness is stressful, non-directed, lacks prioritization, and disrupts focus. It leads to burnout, second guessing, and a general attitude of apathy or distaste related to your goal.

If you find yourself eclipsed by busyness on a given day, the action of preparing for tomorrow will allow you to reset your efforts and refocus your priorities, thereby ensuring that the lack of direction does not continue unfettered.

When To Do It

Perform your Next Day Preparation as one of the last things you do every evening before going to bed.

And once again, please enjoy the resource I created for you through this website:

www.MyMindsetTools.com

Part 35

6. Triggers

What It Is

As a speaker, performer, and guest lecturer, it is not uncommon for me to fly cross-country or even across the Atlantic on a Friday morning, only to be back home by Sunday night.

My wife and stepkids are the undeniable priorities in my life and, if circumstances dictate that they cannot be with me when I travel for work, I seldom stay longer than I need to. I adore seeing the world and feel both grateful and humble that people around the globe want to hear my mindset message in live audiences, but I admit to enjoying the goodnight hugs from my kids much, much more. Providing the highest quality service and commitment to excellence never wanes in me, however, and that is due in large part to enlisting Triggers into my daily schedule several years ago.

Travel had grown to feel burdensome and, regardless of how far I was going or how long I'd be gone, a distinct detachment had started to form in my own mindset. Performing Imagination Theater and Silence every day allowed me to remain connected to my destination and the peace and purpose of my journey, but the exercises proved ineffective in airports, on airplanes, or even in the quietude of a hotel room when the weariness of a travel day had me wanting to do little more than sleep.

Intention Review, Recognition & Appreciation, and Next Day Preparation weren't always pragmatic when bustling through crowded airports and, just like the example above, were often less than appealing at the end of a travel day or after the exhilarating experience of performing in front of a live audience.

Triggers are more passive forms of remaining connected to your Specificity of Intention. Passive, but no less powerful. They can be auditory, visual, or kinesthetic in nature. When used effectively, they can both re-center your conscious thoughts to your goal and your path to its achievement, and reprogram your unconscious dialogue permanently.

Short messages written on cue cards, a specific song or pre-recorded mantra, and an emblem or tiny icon that you either wear or carry with you are all examples of a Trigger.

By listening to, looking at, or touching the Trigger, you provoke a vision and emotion that speaks directly to your Specificity of Intention.

How To Do It

Triggers can and should be used every day of your life, not just on days you find yourself traveling or out of what you'd consider a normal pattern.

My Triggers (three-by-five cue cards) come with me wherever I go, but while I'm at home, they sit right beside me on my desk. At certain points in my day, I purposefully stop what I'm doing and either read the cue cards or simply look at them. When focused and intentional, just the mere act of looking at or touching them reminds me of the goals I have for my life, my Specificity of Intention, and all of the emotion that goes with those visions. In a moment, I can transport myself to the future and literally live in the feeling of what it will be like to achieve it all.

The exercise needn't last more than just a few seconds and doesn't even have to become a formal part of your daily schedule.

I've created both a cue card template as well as incredibly powerful options for Triggers that you can use in your life that will have immediate impact.

Please enjoy the template and the options through this website:

www.MyMindsetTools.com

They are available for immediate access.

Why To Do It

Some days are exhausting.

Some days are scattered.

Some days have unexpected situations arise.

Some days are stressful.

Some days are energizing, completely organized, predictably perfect, and entirely stress-free.

No matter the circumstances or general ambience of your day, having a very quick, accessible method with which to provoke a positive vision and emotion related to your Specificity of Intention will keep you grounded, connected, and working efficiently towards a desired outcome.

When To Do It

Use your Trigger throughout the day as you choose.

And once again, please enjoy the template I created for you through this website:

www.MyMindsetTools.com

Part 36

Perform Imagination Theater for 15-30 minutes every morning.

Use your Trigger for a few minutes throughout the day.

Experience Silence for 15-30 minutes every evening.

Perform your Intention Review, Recognition & Appreciation, and Next Day Preparation in a back-to-back format every evening for a total of 10-15 minutes.

At most, that's seventy-five minutes of your day.

At the minimum, it's a highly effective forty minutes.

Don't let the length of this section convince you that the 6-Pack is somehow hard to understand, difficult to make time for, or challenging to use daily. I wanted to provide you with details and thoroughly explain why each of these exercises are important, how I came to either learn of them or develop them, and the best time to use them each day.

Be sure to take advantage of the additional resources and templates I've provided. They will save you time and allow for immediate implementation of the 6-Pack into your life.

On a final note, please be free to enjoy these exercises however you feel they best fit into your daily schedule. I have created a process based on my experience of teaching the 6-Pack to people around the world and have shared how and when each of the individual exercises seem to have the greatest effect, but there is no need for frustration if that doesn't work for you.

I'm often asked about the best sequence for the 6-Pack. My answer never changes:

The one you'll use every day.

What do you really want...?

SECTION 5: INTENTION

You don't have to see the whole staircase, just take the first step.

—Martin Luther King, Jr.

Part 37

I've always been intrigued by the legend of the half-blind hawk.

A natural predator, one of the hawk's most formidable and deadly assets is the keen eyesight with which it can detect prey from miles away. Even the tiniest mouse scurrying across an open meadow can't go unseen by this lethal hunter.

And the half-blind hawk was no different.

Perched atop the highest tree, it used the vantage point to survey the flat prairies below. Almost effortless and aloof in its analysis of the ground beneath it, the half-blind hawk would sit patiently, waiting for the telltale sign of movement in the short grass.

But unlike other, better-equipped birds of prey, the half-blind hawk wouldn't beeline for the kill. It wouldn't set its sights in a laser-like manner or take a direct trajectory towards the soon-to-be casualty.

It wouldn't, because it couldn't.

Even though gifted with all the innate ability and potential that every other hawk had been awarded at birth, our half-blind friend lacked visual perception. Many believed that this encumbrance would lead to a very short, unfulfilling life. After all, a hawk that lacked perceptive competence couldn't possibly overcome such difficulty and thrive amidst a competitive environment in which every hawk was vying for similar prizes.

Undaunted, the half-blind hawk simply transitioned its apparent weakness into a strength.

It learned, through trial and error, that the only mistaken or unsuccessful attempt was the one it never took. That as long as it got into motion, the exact course or direction needed to achieve the task of trapping its dinner would present itself. Yes, the view from atop the tall tree was both lovely and safe, but also rife with its own dangers. If it were to remain there, the half-blind hawk would die a slow death, never having experienced the rush of flying into the wind or swooping down on its target.

The half-blind hawk didn't know exactly where it was going, but it took specific, intentional flight in order to find out. And that's what made all the difference.

Rather than taking a direct path to its goal—because it really didn't know where that goal was—it simply took flight in faith. It learned to trust that uncertain action was far more valuable than certain inaction; that achieving what it wanted wasn't about being idle until tomorrow so much as getting into deliberate motion today.

Where it was deficient in exactness of detail or path, it was flush with a specificity of intention.

The half-blind hawk would leave the cozy treetop and begin making wide, purposeful circles around the immense plain below. Its sphere-like path would begin focusing on the general vicinity to which it believed the prey was heading. As the wind shifted and created barriers of nuisance, the half-blind hawk simply adjusted its course.

As the now frantic prey attempted to deviate or find cover amongst bushes and shrubbery, the half-blind hawk modified its direction.

It plunged lower and lower. Its circles grew tighter and more specific.

No matter where the prey tried to run, hide, or escape, the half-blind hawk inevitably and masterfully took it down. Every time. It simply took flight with a specificity of intention, without knowing its exact destination or path. The action of getting in motion through faith, while adjusting and modifying as necessary, was all it would ever take to achieve the goal.

Part 38

You are only half-blind because you've yet to uncover yourself.

The actual you.

Behind the layers of influence from a society that demands conformity.

Under the facade of false bravado that cloaks your fears and self-doubts.

Beneath the mask of bravery you've created to ensure that the vulnerability of your own self-loathing would never be seen.

You don't have to tell me that you relate.

Because I know you do.

We all do.

Masks are easy to wear and simple to fashion but challenging to remove, and they come with a cost. The price of real freedom. Not the kind of freedom that ancient religions promise or contemporary politicians try to use as fear tactics to leverage our emotion. The kind that exists within, but very few ever choose to access.

Sawubona means "I see you."

And the sacred agreement of that phrase starts with you. Before we can gain in wealth, we must remove our own limitations of self-worth. Before we can lose weight sustainably, we must abolish our own lingering self-doubt. Before we can find true love, we must curtail our fear to live openly, express authentically, allow others in, and do so in concert with learning to love ourselves fully.

The various influences, experiences, and events that have combined to form your current philosophy of center are a mere mask. This veil hides the true nature of your ability and potential — sometimes from the eyes of others, but always from your own eyes. It's that veil that causes you to idle, forces you to stagnate. Because you feel limited by circumstances or your own faith in yourself. It causes you to second-guess the journey constantly, never free from the grip of fear.

But your philosophy of center is an illusion.

It is a deception that does not represent absolute truth, just the current perspective from which you draw your reality. You do not pursue, because you're uncertain of precisely what the goal is. You do not take flight in faith, because you are unclear of which path to follow.

Yet you will only ever locate the goal and find the path once you step away from those tall trees of comfort and explore.

Specificity of Intention is your compass. Deep down, when you are unburdened by the common strain of over-thinking, you know in rough generalities what you want for your life. When you embrace the Mindset Matters Most ideology, you shift from your current philosophy of center and begin adopting a new imagination of possibility. You calm your fears, nullify your self-doubt, and expand upon your once-held limitations.

Then, you act.

You hold in sight the specificity of your intention, free from the obligation of knowing exactly where it is or how you will achieve it.

Just like our half-blind hawk.

Part 39

The absence of a Specificity of Intention in your life is akin to the absence of the 6-Pack in your days.

You exist as a virtual kite in the most violent of windstorms.

Lacking any degree of strength, support, or stability, you are invariably at the mercy of whichever way the erratic gusts choose to take you. You select one path half-heartedly, only to be blown off-course immediately. Worse yet, you opt for no direction at all and then spend your time reacting to each and every breeze that comes along, regardless of how tepid or turbulent.

The metaphor always reminds me of one of my favorite childhood stories.

One day Alice came to a fork in the road and saw a Cheshire cat in a tree.

"Which road do I take?" she asked.

"Where do you want to go?" was his response.

"I don't know," Alice answered.

"Then," said the cat, "it doesn't matter."

For years, Lewis Carroll's famous passage from *Alice in Wonderland* has struck me as exceptionally powerful. Perhaps Carroll's inspiration is what caused me to become so enthralled with the word "Sawubona" when I first learned of it years ago.

What do you really want?

It's the kind of question that is either considered too spiritually deep to ponder or answered with a superficiality that is based on the general "collective want" influenced by the society we happen to live in.

Have you ever actually reflected on this original question?

"Original" simply because, in a world so rich in resources that help us achieve what we *think* we want, there seems to be a glaring lack of direction in giving us the permission or means to understand what we *really* want.

It's as if our very existences are used for the purpose of "getting there" as quickly as we can, without any real understanding of where "there" is.

Creating your own Specificity of Intention statement is based on two factors:

A single question and a guiding principle.

QUESTION:

In the absence of obstacles, objections, or explicit outcomes, what do I want?

GUIDING PRINCIPLE:

I can't always predict nor control the winds of circumstance and situation, but I can adjust my sails.

Part 40

The question is significantly more powerful than it may at first appear.

Much has been written by success authorities through the years about the absolute need to be definitive in both the exactness of your goal and your plan to achieve it. But in my experience, neither is required. Moreover, they often create the very inaction that prevents people from taking a first step in faith.

You don't always know exactly what you want, where you're going, or how to get yourself there, and you never will unless you create momentum through intended action. The art of Silence is an essential element to help unlock streams of creativity that begin shaping and guiding the direction of your journey. But it alone is far too passive an exercise to reveal the path if unaccompanied by movement.

Being half-blind due to your lack of intimacy with self, or uncertainty in the exactness of your destination, does not handicap your potential for success. It simply means that large, looping circles must be made towards a specific intention in faith. It means that, as you draw closer and closer to the objective, you trust your path to become increasingly more certain and direct.

Diminish the obstacles you may see in your current situation or circumstances.

Restrict the objections that creep in from your thoughts, which likely still swim in oceans of limitation, self-doubt, and fear.

Reduce your need to know the precise nature of the outcome.

And from that state, decide what you want.

Write it down.

That is your Specificity of Intention.

Part 41

The Guiding Principle is equally important.

Life comes with no situational guarantees. There are no certainties or security, no matter how much planning and forecasting is brought to the equation. But if we choose to flow with the waxing and waning rather than resist the natural oscillation of life, we find that barriers are mere matters of perception; obstacles are fluid in texture and only as prohibitive as we interpret them to be.

One of the many definitions of Dharma in Buddhism is "the state of nature as it is." I've long drawn a connection to Dharma, both conceptually and as it relates to the act of flowing along my own journey. There is great complexity to the harmony of nature, but within its intricate and delicate balance, simplicity reigns.

Nature just works.

When barriers present themselves, it finds a way.

When obstacles arise, it finds a means.

It does not sit still and contemplate where it should go, fret about how it should get there, or wonder if it's worthy. It moves in faith. It trusts that all necessary ways and means will be made visible as the result of intentional action.

That's you when living within Dharma.

Forever remember our half-blind hawk:

"The action of getting in motion through faith, while adjusting and modifying as necessary, is all it will ever take to achieve your goal."

Part 42

Some leaders tell you what to do.

How to do it.

Why you should do it the way they think is best.

And why you are very, very wrong if you don't agree.

I never wanted to have that kind of voice.

I will continue the journey of finding freedom within myself...

...and in doing so, I hope to help you find your own freedom within you.

ABOUT THE AUTHOR

Brian has worked as a mindset mentor and consultant to elite athletes, corporate executives, entrepreneurs, and life-seekers from around the world.

Learn more about him and his mindset mentorship opportunities at:

www.BrianGrasso.com

Health, Wellness, Fitness, Business & Life Coaches...

...Become a "Certified Mindset Specialist" Today:

www.MindsetPerformanceInstitute.com

Made in the USA
San Bernardino, CA
16 May 2017